50 Whiskey in the Kitchen Recipes

By: Kelly Johnson

Table of Contents

- Whisky Glazed Salmon
- Whisky BBQ Ribs
- Whisky Mushroom Risotto
- Whisky Mac and Cheese
- Whisky and Maple Glazed Carrots
- Whisky Chicken Marinade
- Whisky-Infused Beef Stew
- Whisky Sour Chicken Wings
- Whisky-Soaked Fruitcake
- Whisky Chocolate Sauce
- Whisky BBQ Sauce
- Whisky Balsamic Vinaigrette
- Whisky Mashed Sweet Potatoes
- Whisky-Caramel Bread Pudding
- Whisky Marinade for Grilled Shrimp
- Whisky-Cream Sauce for Pasta
- Whisky Pumpkin Pie
- Whisky and Honey Glazed Ham
- Whisky Chocolate Truffles
- Whisky-Infused Chilli
- Whisky-Glazed Brussels Sprouts
- Whisky Baked Apples
- Whisky Barbecue Meatballs
- Whisky and Orange Glazed Duck
- Whisky-Infused Risotto with Peas
- Whisky Lemonade Chicken
- Whisky-Infused BBQ Pulled Pork
- Whisky-Candied Bacon
- Whisky Cranberry Sauce
- Whisky-Glazed Pork Tenderloin
- Whisky-Infused Chili Cornbread
- Whisky Caramel Sauce for Ice Cream
- Whisky and Herb Roasted Chicken
- Whisky-Infused Stuffing
- Whisky Maple Glazed Brussels Sprouts
- Whisky-Soaked Pancakes

- Whisky-Infused Tomato Sauce
- Whisky Barbecue Pulled Jackfruit
- Whisky-Glazed Roasted Vegetables
- Whisky and Ginger Marinated Steak
- Whisky Bread Pudding
- Whisky-Infused Rice Pudding
- Whisky-Lemon Baked Chicken
- Whisky-Glazed Tofu
- Whisky Infused Hot Chocolate
- Whisky and Black Pepper Pork Chops
- Whisky Cranberry Chicken
- Whisky BBQ Cauliflower Bites
- Whisky-Infused Chocolate Cake
- Whisky-Peach Glazed Chicken

Whisky Glazed Salmon

Ingredients:

- 4 salmon fillets
- 1/4 cup whisky
- 1/4 cup brown sugar
- 2 tbsp soy sauce
- 1 tbsp Dijon mustard
- Salt and pepper to taste

Instructions:

1. In a small saucepan, combine whisky, brown sugar, soy sauce, and Dijon mustard. Simmer until thickened.
2. Preheat grill or oven to medium-high heat.
3. Season salmon with salt and pepper. Brush with the glaze.
4. Grill or bake salmon for 6-8 minutes per side, brushing with more glaze during cooking.

Whisky BBQ Ribs

Ingredients:

- 2 racks of pork ribs
- 1/2 cup whisky
- 1 cup BBQ sauce
- 2 tbsp brown sugar
- 1 tbsp smoked paprika
- Salt and pepper to taste

Instructions:

1. Preheat oven to 300°F (150°C).
2. In a bowl, mix whisky, BBQ sauce, brown sugar, smoked paprika, salt, and pepper.
3. Rub ribs with the mixture and place on a baking sheet. Cover with foil.
4. Bake for 2-3 hours, then remove foil and grill for 10-15 minutes for a charred finish.

Whisky Mushroom Risotto

Ingredients:

- 1 cup Arborio rice
- 4 cups chicken or vegetable broth
- 1 cup mushrooms, sliced
- 1/2 cup whisky
- 1 small onion, diced
- 2 cloves garlic, minced
- 1/2 cup grated Parmesan cheese
- 2 tbsp butter
- Salt and pepper to taste

Instructions:

1. In a saucepan, heat broth and keep warm.
2. In a large skillet, melt butter, and sauté onion and garlic until translucent.
3. Add mushrooms and cook until tender.
4. Stir in Arborio rice and toast for 1-2 minutes.
5. Add whisky and cook until absorbed. Gradually add warm broth, one ladle at a time, stirring until absorbed.
6. Stir in Parmesan cheese, salt, and pepper before serving.

Whisky Mac and Cheese

Ingredients:

- 8 oz macaroni
- 2 cups shredded cheddar cheese
- 1/2 cup whisky
- 1/4 cup milk
- 1/4 cup breadcrumbs
- 2 tbsp butter
- Salt and pepper to taste

Instructions:

1. Cook macaroni according to package instructions. Drain.
2. In a saucepan, melt butter, and stir in whisky and milk.
3. Add cheese, stirring until melted. Mix in macaroni, salt, and pepper.
4. Transfer to a baking dish, top with breadcrumbs, and bake at 350°F (175°C) for 20 minutes.

Whisky and Maple Glazed Carrots

Ingredients:

- 1 lb carrots, sliced
- 1/4 cup whisky
- 1/4 cup maple syrup
- 2 tbsp butter
- Salt and pepper to taste

Instructions:

1. In a skillet, melt butter and add whisky and maple syrup.
2. Add sliced carrots and cook until tender, about 10-15 minutes.
3. Season with salt and pepper before serving.

Whisky Chicken Marinade

Ingredients:

- 1/2 cup whisky
- 1/4 cup soy sauce
- 1/4 cup olive oil
- 2 tbsp brown sugar
- 2 cloves garlic, minced
- Salt and pepper to taste

Instructions:

1. In a bowl, mix whisky, soy sauce, olive oil, brown sugar, garlic, salt, and pepper.
2. Marinate chicken for at least 1 hour before cooking.

Whisky-Infused Beef Stew

Ingredients:

- 2 lbs beef chuck, cubed
- 1 cup whisky
- 4 cups beef broth
- 2 cups vegetables (carrots, potatoes, etc.)
- 1 onion, diced
- 2 cloves garlic, minced
- Salt and pepper to taste

Instructions:

1. In a large pot, brown beef cubes.
2. Add onions and garlic, cooking until soft.
3. Stir in whisky and deglaze the pot.
4. Add broth and vegetables, then simmer for 2-3 hours until beef is tender.

Whisky Sour Chicken Wings

Ingredients:

- 2 lbs chicken wings
- 1/4 cup whisky
- 1/4 cup lemon juice
- 1/4 cup honey
- Salt and pepper to taste

Instructions:

1. In a bowl, mix whisky, lemon juice, honey, salt, and pepper.
2. Marinate wings for at least 1 hour.
3. Bake wings at 400°F (200°C) for 25-30 minutes, turning halfway.
4. Toss wings in remaining marinade before serving.

Whisky-Soaked Fruitcake

Ingredients:

- 2 cups mixed dried fruits (raisins, cherries, apricots)
- 1 cup whisky
- 1 1/2 cups all-purpose flour
- 1 tsp baking powder
- 1/2 tsp salt
- 1 tsp ground cinnamon
- 1/2 cup unsalted butter, softened
- 1 cup brown sugar
- 3 large eggs
- 1/2 cup chopped nuts (optional)

Instructions:

1. Soak dried fruits in whisky for at least 4 hours or overnight.
2. Preheat oven to 325°F (160°C) and grease a loaf pan.
3. In a bowl, mix flour, baking powder, salt, and cinnamon.
4. In another bowl, cream butter and brown sugar until fluffy. Add eggs one at a time.
5. Gradually add dry ingredients, mixing well. Fold in soaked fruits and nuts.
6. Pour into the prepared loaf pan and bake for 1 hour, or until a toothpick comes out clean.

Whisky Chocolate Sauce

Ingredients:

- 1 cup dark chocolate chips
- 1/2 cup heavy cream
- 1/4 cup whisky
- 1 tbsp butter
- Pinch of salt

Instructions:

1. In a saucepan, heat heavy cream until just boiling.
2. Remove from heat and stir in chocolate chips until melted and smooth.
3. Add whisky, butter, and salt, stirring until well combined.
4. Serve warm over ice cream or desserts.

Whisky BBQ Sauce

Ingredients:

- 1 cup ketchup
- 1/4 cup whisky
- 1/4 cup apple cider vinegar
- 1/4 cup brown sugar
- 1 tbsp Worcestershire sauce
- 1 tsp smoked paprika
- Salt and pepper to taste

Instructions:

1. In a saucepan, combine all ingredients over medium heat.
2. Simmer for 15-20 minutes, stirring occasionally, until thickened.
3. Use as a glaze or dipping sauce for meats.

Whisky Balsamic Vinaigrette

Ingredients:

- 1/4 cup balsamic vinegar
- 1/4 cup whisky
- 1/2 cup olive oil
- 1 tsp Dijon mustard
- Salt and pepper to taste

Instructions:

1. In a bowl, whisk together balsamic vinegar, whisky, Dijon mustard, salt, and pepper.
2. Gradually add olive oil, whisking until emulsified.
3. Serve over salads or grilled vegetables.

Whisky Mashed Sweet Potatoes

Ingredients:

- 2 lbs sweet potatoes, peeled and cubed
- 1/4 cup whisky
- 1/4 cup heavy cream
- 2 tbsp butter
- Salt and pepper to taste

Instructions:

1. Boil sweet potatoes until tender, about 15-20 minutes. Drain and return to pot.
2. Mash sweet potatoes, then stir in whisky, heavy cream, butter, salt, and pepper until smooth.

Whisky-Caramel Bread Pudding

Ingredients:

- 4 cups cubed bread (stale or toasted)
- 2 cups milk
- 1/2 cup sugar
- 4 eggs
- 1/2 cup whisky
- 1 tsp vanilla extract
- 1/2 cup caramel sauce

Instructions:

1. Preheat oven to 350°F (175°C) and grease a baking dish.
2. In a bowl, whisk together milk, sugar, eggs, whisky, and vanilla.
3. Stir in bread cubes and let soak for 15 minutes.
4. Pour mixture into the baking dish and drizzle with caramel sauce.
5. Bake for 40-45 minutes, or until set and golden.

Whisky Marinade for Grilled Shrimp

Ingredients:

- 1/4 cup whisky
- 2 tbsp olive oil
- 2 tbsp lemon juice
- 2 cloves garlic, minced
- Salt and pepper to taste
- 1 lb shrimp, peeled and deveined

Instructions:

1. In a bowl, mix whisky, olive oil, lemon juice, garlic, salt, and pepper.
2. Add shrimp, coating well, and marinate for 30 minutes.
3. Grill shrimp over medium heat for 2-3 minutes per side until cooked through.

Whisky-Cream Sauce for Pasta

Ingredients:

- 1 cup heavy cream
- 1/4 cup whisky
- 1/2 cup grated Parmesan cheese
- 1 tbsp butter
- Salt and pepper to taste
- Cooked pasta of choice

Instructions:

1. In a saucepan, melt butter over medium heat.
2. Add whisky and simmer for 2-3 minutes.
3. Stir in heavy cream and Parmesan, cooking until thickened.
4. Season with salt and pepper, then toss with cooked pasta.

Whisky Pumpkin Pie

Ingredients:

- 1 unbaked pie crust
- 1 can (15 oz) pumpkin puree
- 3/4 cup sugar
- 1/2 tsp salt
- 1 tsp ground cinnamon
- 1/2 tsp ground nutmeg
- 1/4 tsp ground ginger
- 3 large eggs
- 1 cup heavy cream
- 1/4 cup whisky

Instructions:

1. Preheat oven to 425°F (220°C).
2. In a mixing bowl, combine pumpkin puree, sugar, salt, spices, and eggs.
3. Gradually stir in heavy cream and whisky until smooth.
4. Pour the filling into the pie crust and bake for 15 minutes.
5. Reduce temperature to 350°F (175°C) and bake for an additional 35-40 minutes, or until set. Let cool before serving.

Whisky and Honey Glazed Ham

Ingredients:

- 1 fully cooked ham (about 8-10 lbs)
- 1/2 cup whisky
- 1/2 cup honey
- 1/4 cup brown sugar
- 2 tbsp Dijon mustard
- 1/2 tsp ground cloves

Instructions:

1. Preheat oven to 325°F (160°C).
2. In a saucepan, combine whisky, honey, brown sugar, mustard, and cloves. Bring to a simmer until thickened.
3. Place the ham in a roasting pan and brush with the glaze.
4. Bake for 1.5 to 2 hours, basting with glaze every 30 minutes, until heated through and caramelized.

Whisky Chocolate Truffles

Ingredients:

- 8 oz dark chocolate, chopped
- 1/2 cup heavy cream
- 2 tbsp whisky
- Cocoa powder for dusting

Instructions:

1. In a saucepan, heat heavy cream until simmering.
2. Pour over chopped chocolate and let sit for a minute, then stir until smooth.
3. Stir in whisky and refrigerate for about 2 hours until firm.
4. Scoop out small amounts and roll into balls, then coat in cocoa powder.

Whisky-Infused Chilli

Ingredients:

- 1 lb ground beef or turkey
- 1 onion, chopped
- 2 cloves garlic, minced
- 1 bell pepper, chopped
- 1 can (14 oz) diced tomatoes
- 1 can (15 oz) kidney beans, drained
- 1 cup whisky
- 2 tbsp chili powder
- 1 tsp cumin
- Salt and pepper to taste

Instructions:

1. In a large pot, brown the ground meat over medium heat.
2. Add onion, garlic, and bell pepper; cook until softened.
3. Stir in diced tomatoes, kidney beans, whisky, chili powder, cumin, salt, and pepper.
4. Simmer for 30-40 minutes, stirring occasionally, until thickened.

Whisky-Glazed Brussels Sprouts

Ingredients:

- 1 lb Brussels sprouts, halved
- 1/4 cup whisky
- 1/4 cup balsamic vinegar
- 2 tbsp honey
- 2 tbsp olive oil
- Salt and pepper to taste

Instructions:

1. Preheat oven to 400°F (200°C).
2. In a bowl, whisk together whisky, balsamic vinegar, honey, olive oil, salt, and pepper.
3. Toss Brussels sprouts in the mixture and spread on a baking sheet.
4. Roast for 20-25 minutes until tender and caramelized, stirring halfway through.

Whisky Baked Apples

Ingredients:

- 4 medium apples, cored
- 1/4 cup whisky
- 1/4 cup brown sugar
- 1/4 tsp cinnamon
- 1/4 cup raisins (optional)
- 1/4 cup chopped nuts (optional)

Instructions:

1. Preheat oven to 350°F (175°C).
2. Place cored apples in a baking dish.
3. In a bowl, mix whisky, brown sugar, cinnamon, raisins, and nuts.
4. Spoon mixture into the apples and pour remaining liquid over them.
5. Bake for 25-30 minutes until tender.

Whisky Barbecue Meatballs

Ingredients:

- 1 lb ground beef or turkey
- 1/2 cup breadcrumbs
- 1/4 cup grated Parmesan cheese
- 1 egg
- 1/4 cup whisky
- 1 cup barbecue sauce

Instructions:

1. Preheat oven to 375°F (190°C).
2. In a bowl, combine meat, breadcrumbs, Parmesan, egg, whisky, salt, and pepper.
3. Form into meatballs and place on a baking sheet.
4. Bake for 20-25 minutes until cooked through.
5. Toss with barbecue sauce and serve.

Whisky and Orange Glazed Duck

Ingredients:

- 1 whole duck (about 4-5 lbs)
- 1/2 cup whisky
- 1/2 cup orange juice
- 1/4 cup honey
- 1 tbsp soy sauce
- Salt and pepper to taste

Instructions:

1. Preheat oven to 350°F (175°C).
2. In a bowl, mix whisky, orange juice, honey, soy sauce, salt, and pepper.
3. Place duck in a roasting pan and brush with glaze.
4. Roast for 1.5 to 2 hours, basting every 30 minutes until skin is crispy and duck is cooked through.

Whisky-Infused Risotto with Peas

Ingredients:

- 1 cup Arborio rice
- 4 cups chicken or vegetable broth
- 1/2 cup whisky
- 1 small onion, finely chopped
- 2 cloves garlic, minced
- 1 cup frozen peas
- 1/2 cup grated Parmesan cheese
- 2 tbsp olive oil
- Salt and pepper to taste
- Fresh parsley for garnish

Instructions:

1. In a saucepan, heat the broth and keep it warm over low heat.
2. In a large skillet, heat olive oil over medium heat. Add onion and garlic; sauté until translucent.
3. Stir in the Arborio rice and cook for 1-2 minutes until lightly toasted.
4. Pour in the whisky and stir until absorbed.
5. Gradually add warm broth, one ladle at a time, stirring frequently until absorbed before adding more.
6. After about 15-20 minutes, when the rice is creamy and al dente, stir in peas and Parmesan. Season with salt and pepper.
7. Garnish with fresh parsley before serving.

Whisky Lemonade Chicken

Ingredients:

- 4 boneless chicken breasts
- 1/2 cup whisky
- 1/2 cup lemonade
- 1/4 cup soy sauce
- 2 tbsp olive oil
- 2 cloves garlic, minced
- Salt and pepper to taste

Instructions:

1. In a bowl, whisk together whisky, lemonade, soy sauce, olive oil, garlic, salt, and pepper.
2. Place chicken breasts in a resealable bag and pour marinade over them. Seal and refrigerate for at least 1 hour (or overnight).
3. Preheat grill or skillet over medium-high heat.
4. Remove chicken from marinade and cook for 6-7 minutes on each side or until cooked through.
5. Serve with your choice of sides.

Whisky-Infused BBQ Pulled Pork

Ingredients:

- 3 lbs pork shoulder
- 1/2 cup whisky
- 1 cup BBQ sauce
- 1 onion, chopped
- 3 cloves garlic, minced
- 1 tbsp paprika
- 1 tbsp brown sugar
- Salt and pepper to taste

Instructions:

1. In a slow cooker, combine whisky, BBQ sauce, onion, garlic, paprika, brown sugar, salt, and pepper.
2. Add the pork shoulder, ensuring it's well coated with the sauce.
3. Cover and cook on low for 8-10 hours, until tender.
4. Shred the pork with forks and mix with the sauce.
5. Serve on buns or with sides of your choice.

Whisky-Candied Bacon

Ingredients:

- 1 lb thick-cut bacon
- 1/2 cup brown sugar
- 1/4 cup whisky
- 1/4 tsp black pepper

Instructions:

1. Preheat oven to 350°F (175°C).
2. In a bowl, mix brown sugar, whisky, and black pepper.
3. Lay bacon strips on a baking sheet lined with parchment paper.
4. Brush the whisky mixture over the bacon.
5. Bake for 20-25 minutes, until crispy and caramelized, flipping halfway through.
6. Let cool before serving.

Whisky Cranberry Sauce

Ingredients:

- 12 oz fresh cranberries
- 1 cup sugar
- 1 cup water
- 1/2 cup whisky
- Zest of 1 orange

Instructions:

1. In a saucepan, combine water, sugar, and cranberries. Bring to a boil.
2. Reduce heat and simmer for about 10 minutes, until cranberries burst.
3. Stir in whisky and orange zest.
4. Remove from heat and let cool. The sauce will thicken as it cools.

Whisky-Glazed Pork Tenderloin

Ingredients:

- 1-2 lbs pork tenderloin
- 1/2 cup whisky
- 1/4 cup brown sugar
- 1/4 cup soy sauce
- 2 cloves garlic, minced
- 1 tsp mustard
- Salt and pepper to taste

Instructions:

1. Preheat oven to 375°F (190°C).
2. In a bowl, whisk together whisky, brown sugar, soy sauce, garlic, mustard, salt, and pepper.
3. Place pork tenderloin in a baking dish and pour marinade over it.
4. Bake for 25-30 minutes, basting with the sauce halfway through, until the internal temperature reaches 145°F (63°C).
5. Let rest for 5-10 minutes before slicing.

Whisky-Infused Chili Cornbread

Ingredients:

- 1 cup cornmeal
- 1 cup all-purpose flour
- 1/4 cup sugar
- 1 tbsp baking powder
- 1 cup milk
- 1/4 cup whisky
- 1/4 cup melted butter
- 1 can (15 oz) chili (optional)
- 1 cup shredded cheddar cheese

Instructions:

1. Preheat oven to 400°F (200°C).
2. In a bowl, mix cornmeal, flour, sugar, and baking powder.
3. In another bowl, combine milk, whisky, and melted butter.
4. Pour the wet ingredients into the dry and mix until just combined.
5. Fold in chili and cheese, if using.
6. Pour into a greased baking dish and bake for 20-25 minutes until golden.

Whisky Caramel Sauce for Ice Cream

Ingredients:

- 1 cup sugar
- 1/4 cup water
- 1/2 cup heavy cream
- 1/4 cup whisky
- 1/4 cup butter
- 1/2 tsp salt

Instructions:

1. In a saucepan, combine sugar and water over medium heat. Stir until sugar dissolves.
2. Let it boil without stirring until it turns a deep amber color (about 10 minutes).
3. Carefully whisk in heavy cream (it will bubble), then add whisky, butter, and salt.
4. Remove from heat and let cool slightly before serving over ice cream.

Whisky and Herb Roasted Chicken

Ingredients:

- 1 whole chicken (about 4-5 lbs)
- 1/2 cup whisky
- 2 tbsp olive oil
- 2 tbsp fresh rosemary, chopped
- 2 tbsp fresh thyme, chopped
- 4 cloves garlic, minced
- Salt and pepper to taste
- 1 lemon, halved

Instructions:

1. Preheat your oven to 375°F (190°C).
2. In a bowl, mix whisky, olive oil, rosemary, thyme, garlic, salt, and pepper.
3. Pat the chicken dry and rub the whisky mixture all over the chicken, including under the skin.
4. Place lemon halves inside the cavity of the chicken.
5. Roast in the oven for about 1.5 hours or until the internal temperature reaches 165°F (74°C).
6. Let it rest for 10 minutes before carving and serving.

Whisky-Infused Stuffing

Ingredients:

- 1 loaf of bread, cubed (about 8 cups)
- 1/2 cup whisky
- 1/2 cup chicken broth
- 1 onion, chopped
- 2 celery stalks, chopped
- 2 cloves garlic, minced
- 1 tsp dried sage
- 1 tsp dried thyme
- Salt and pepper to taste
- 1/4 cup butter

Instructions:

1. Preheat your oven to 350°F (175°C).
2. In a skillet, melt butter over medium heat. Add onion, celery, and garlic; sauté until soft.
3. In a large bowl, combine bread cubes, sautéed vegetables, whisky, chicken broth, sage, thyme, salt, and pepper.
4. Mix until well combined, then transfer to a greased baking dish.
5. Bake for 30-35 minutes until golden and crispy on top.

Whisky Maple Glazed Brussels Sprouts

Ingredients:

- 1 lb Brussels sprouts, halved
- 1/4 cup whisky
- 1/4 cup maple syrup
- 2 tbsp olive oil
- Salt and pepper to taste

Instructions:

1. Preheat your oven to 400°F (200°C).
2. In a large bowl, toss Brussels sprouts with olive oil, salt, and pepper.
3. Spread on a baking sheet and roast for 20 minutes.
4. In a small saucepan, combine whisky and maple syrup; simmer until slightly thickened.
5. Drizzle the whisky glaze over the Brussels sprouts and roast for an additional 10 minutes.

Whisky-Soaked Pancakes

Ingredients:

- 1 cup all-purpose flour
- 2 tbsp sugar
- 1 tbsp baking powder
- 1/2 tsp salt
- 1 cup milk
- 1/4 cup whisky
- 1 large egg
- 2 tbsp melted butter

Instructions:

1. In a bowl, whisk together flour, sugar, baking powder, and salt.
2. In another bowl, mix milk, whisky, egg, and melted butter.
3. Combine wet and dry ingredients until just mixed (lumps are okay).
4. Heat a griddle or skillet over medium heat and pour 1/4 cup of batter for each pancake.
5. Cook until bubbles form, then flip and cook until golden brown.

Whisky-Infused Tomato Sauce

Ingredients:

- 1 can (28 oz) crushed tomatoes
- 1/2 cup whisky
- 1 onion, chopped
- 3 cloves garlic, minced
- 1 tsp dried oregano
- 1 tsp sugar
- Salt and pepper to taste
- 2 tbsp olive oil

Instructions:

1. In a saucepan, heat olive oil over medium heat. Add onion and garlic; sauté until softened.
2. Stir in crushed tomatoes, whisky, oregano, sugar, salt, and pepper.
3. Bring to a simmer and cook for 20-30 minutes, stirring occasionally, until thickened.

Whisky Barbecue Pulled Jackfruit

Ingredients:

- 2 cans young green jackfruit in water (drained and rinsed)
- 1/2 cup whisky
- 1 cup BBQ sauce
- 1 onion, chopped
- 2 cloves garlic, minced
- 1 tsp smoked paprika
- 1 tbsp olive oil

Instructions:

1. In a skillet, heat olive oil over medium heat. Add onion and garlic; sauté until soft.
2. Add jackfruit and cook for a few minutes, then stir in whisky, BBQ sauce, and smoked paprika.
3. Simmer for 20 minutes, then shred the jackfruit with forks.
4. Serve on buns or with sides.

Whisky-Glazed Roasted Vegetables

Ingredients:

- 4 cups mixed vegetables (carrots, bell peppers, zucchini, etc.)
- 1/4 cup whisky
- 1/4 cup balsamic vinegar
- 2 tbsp olive oil
- Salt and pepper to taste
- Fresh herbs for garnish

Instructions:

1. Preheat oven to 425°F (220°C).
2. In a bowl, mix whisky, balsamic vinegar, olive oil, salt, and pepper.
3. Toss vegetables in the whisky mixture until coated.
4. Spread on a baking sheet and roast for 25-30 minutes, stirring halfway through.
5. Garnish with fresh herbs before serving.

Whisky and Ginger Marinated Steak

Ingredients:

- 2 ribeye steaks
- 1/4 cup whisky
- 1/4 cup soy sauce
- 2 tbsp fresh ginger, grated
- 2 cloves garlic, minced
- 1 tbsp olive oil
- Salt and pepper to taste

Instructions:

1. In a bowl, whisk together whisky, soy sauce, ginger, garlic, olive oil, salt, and pepper.
2. Place steaks in a resealable bag and pour the marinade over them. Seal and refrigerate for at least 1 hour (or overnight).
3. Preheat grill or skillet over high heat.
4. Remove steaks from marinade and cook to desired doneness. Let rest before slicing.

Whisky Bread Pudding

Ingredients:

- 4 cups cubed day-old bread
- 1/2 cup whisky
- 2 cups milk
- 1/2 cup sugar
- 4 large eggs
- 1 tsp vanilla extract
- 1 tsp ground cinnamon
- 1/2 cup raisins (optional)
- 1/4 cup butter, melted

Instructions:

1. Preheat your oven to 350°F (175°C).
2. In a bowl, mix whisky, milk, sugar, eggs, vanilla, and cinnamon until well combined.
3. In a greased baking dish, layer the bread cubes and raisins.
4. Pour the whisky mixture over the bread, ensuring all pieces are soaked.
5. Drizzle melted butter on top.
6. Bake for 45-50 minutes or until set and golden. Let it cool before serving.

Whisky-Infused Rice Pudding

Ingredients:

- 1 cup arborio rice
- 4 cups milk
- 1/2 cup sugar
- 1/4 cup whisky
- 1 tsp vanilla extract
- 1/2 tsp ground cinnamon
- Pinch of salt
- Raisins or chopped nuts for garnish (optional)

Instructions:

1. In a saucepan, combine rice, milk, sugar, and salt. Bring to a simmer over medium heat, stirring frequently.
2. Cook until the rice is tender and the mixture thickens, about 20-25 minutes.
3. Stir in whisky, vanilla, and cinnamon.
4. Remove from heat and let it cool slightly before serving. Garnish with raisins or nuts if desired.

Whisky-Lemon Baked Chicken

Ingredients:

- 4 chicken breasts
- 1/2 cup whisky
- Juice and zest of 1 lemon
- 2 tbsp olive oil
- 2 cloves garlic, minced
- Salt and pepper to taste
- Fresh parsley for garnish

Instructions:

1. Preheat your oven to 375°F (190°C).
2. In a bowl, whisk together whisky, lemon juice, lemon zest, olive oil, garlic, salt, and pepper.
3. Place chicken breasts in a baking dish and pour the marinade over them.
4. Bake for 25-30 minutes or until the chicken is cooked through.
5. Garnish with fresh parsley before serving.

Whisky-Glazed Tofu

Ingredients:

- 1 block firm tofu, drained and pressed
- 1/4 cup whisky
- 1/4 cup soy sauce
- 2 tbsp maple syrup
- 1 tbsp rice vinegar
- 1 tbsp sesame oil
- 2 green onions, sliced

Instructions:

1. Cut tofu into cubes and set aside.
2. In a bowl, whisk together whisky, soy sauce, maple syrup, rice vinegar, and sesame oil.
3. In a skillet over medium heat, add tofu and cook until golden brown on all sides.
4. Pour the whisky mixture over the tofu and cook until the glaze thickens, about 5 minutes.
5. Garnish with sliced green onions before serving.

Whisky Infused Hot Chocolate

Ingredients:

- 2 cups milk
- 1/4 cup heavy cream
- 1/4 cup whisky
- 2 tbsp unsweetened cocoa powder
- 2 tbsp sugar
- 1/2 tsp vanilla extract
- Whipped cream for topping

Instructions:

1. In a saucepan, heat milk and cream over medium heat until warm.
2. Whisk in cocoa powder and sugar until fully dissolved.
3. Remove from heat and stir in whisky and vanilla.
4. Serve in mugs topped with whipped cream.

Whisky and Black Pepper Pork Chops

Ingredients:

- 4 pork chops
- 1/4 cup whisky
- 2 tbsp soy sauce
- 1 tbsp black pepper
- 2 cloves garlic, minced
- 1 tbsp olive oil

Instructions:

1. In a bowl, mix whisky, soy sauce, black pepper, and garlic.
2. Marinate pork chops in the mixture for at least 30 minutes.
3. In a skillet, heat olive oil over medium-high heat.
4. Cook pork chops for 5-7 minutes per side or until cooked through.
5. Let rest before serving.

Whisky Cranberry Chicken

Ingredients:

- 4 chicken thighs
- 1 cup cranberry juice
- 1/4 cup whisky
- 2 tbsp brown sugar
- 1 tsp dried thyme
- Salt and pepper to taste

Instructions:

1. Preheat your oven to 350°F (175°C).
2. In a bowl, mix cranberry juice, whisky, brown sugar, thyme, salt, and pepper.
3. Place chicken thighs in a baking dish and pour the cranberry mixture over them.
4. Bake for 35-40 minutes or until the chicken is cooked through.
5. Serve with the sauce drizzled on top.

Whisky BBQ Cauliflower Bites

Ingredients:

- 1 head cauliflower, cut into florets
- 1/4 cup whisky
- 1/4 cup BBQ sauce
- 2 tbsp olive oil
- Salt and pepper to taste

Instructions:

1. Preheat your oven to 425°F (220°C).
2. In a bowl, mix whisky, BBQ sauce, olive oil, salt, and pepper.
3. Toss cauliflower florets in the mixture until well coated.
4. Spread on a baking sheet and roast for 20-25 minutes, until golden and tender.
5. Serve hot as a side or snack.

Whisky-Infused Chocolate Cake

Ingredients:

- **For the Cake:**
    - 1 ¾ cups all-purpose flour
    - 1 ¾ cups granulated sugar
    - ¾ cup unsweetened cocoa powder
    - 1 ½ tsp baking powder
    - 1 ½ tsp baking soda
    - 1 tsp salt
    - 2 large eggs
    - 1 cup whole milk
    - ½ cup vegetable oil
    - 2 tsp vanilla extract
    - 1 cup boiling water
    - ½ cup whisky
- **For the Whisky Ganache:**
    - 1 cup heavy cream
    - 8 oz semi-sweet chocolate, chopped
    - 2 tbsp whisky
    - 1 tsp vanilla extract

Instructions:

1. **Prepare the Cake:**
    - Preheat your oven to 350°F (175°C). Grease and flour two 9-inch round cake pans.
    - In a large mixing bowl, combine the flour, sugar, cocoa powder, baking powder, baking soda, and salt.
    - Add the eggs, milk, vegetable oil, and vanilla extract. Mix on medium speed for 2 minutes until well combined.
    - Carefully stir in the boiling water and whisky. The batter will be thin.
    - Pour the batter evenly into the prepared cake pans and bake for 30-35 minutes or until a toothpick inserted into the center comes out clean.
    - Allow the cakes to cool in the pans for 10 minutes, then remove them from the pans and cool completely on wire racks.
2. **Prepare the Ganache:**
    - In a small saucepan, heat the heavy cream over medium heat until it just begins to simmer.
    - Remove from heat and add the chopped chocolate. Let it sit for 5 minutes, then stir until smooth.
    - Stir in the whisky and vanilla extract. Allow the ganache to cool until it thickens slightly.
3. **Assemble the Cake:**

- Place one cake layer on a serving plate. Spread a layer of ganache on top.
- Place the second cake layer on top and pour the remaining ganache over the top, allowing it to drip down the sides.
- Let the ganache set before serving.

Whisky-Peach Glazed Chicken

Ingredients:

- 4 boneless, skinless chicken breasts
- 1 cup peach preserves
- 1/4 cup whisky
- 2 tbsp soy sauce
- 1 tbsp Dijon mustard
- 1 tsp garlic powder
- 1 tsp onion powder
- Salt and pepper to taste
- Fresh peach slices for garnish (optional)
- Chopped parsley for garnish (optional)

Instructions:

1. **Prepare the Marinade:**
    - In a bowl, whisk together peach preserves, whisky, soy sauce, Dijon mustard, garlic powder, onion powder, salt, and pepper.
    - Reserve half of the marinade for later use.
2. **Marinate the Chicken:**
    - Place the chicken breasts in a resealable plastic bag or shallow dish. Pour the marinade over the chicken and ensure it is well-coated.
    - Marinate in the refrigerator for at least 30 minutes, or up to 4 hours for more flavor.
3. **Cook the Chicken:**
    - Preheat your grill or skillet over medium-high heat.
    - Remove the chicken from the marinade and discard the used marinade.
    - Grill or cook the chicken for about 6-7 minutes per side, or until the chicken is cooked through and reaches an internal temperature of 165°F (75°C).
    - During the last few minutes of cooking, brush the reserved marinade over the chicken for added flavor.
4. **Serve:**
    - Remove the chicken from the heat and let it rest for a few minutes.
    - Slice the chicken and serve with fresh peach slices and a sprinkle of chopped parsley, if desired.

www.ingramcontent.com/pod-product-compliance
Lightning Source LLC
LaVergne TN
LVHW081329060526
838201LV00055B/2544